Introduction:

Con-Science, a play on words, on the word, that so explicitly and blatantly sums up all perception by a sentient being of everything that's around him/her or it, with a completely vague moral and ethical context whose borders divulge into each other or more so, their existence is in such a way that undoes another's, with all the dilemmatic quandary that shrouds the empirical reality into confines of the observer, but what actually is conscience that our beings are so conscious of, the trivial matter that governs all actions which are supported by a complex working of organ systems, as all these organs have been in influenced by the changes in their previous method of task execution, in a like manner, the conscience itself has adapted or at least the frame work thereof, by the actions, thoughts and hopes of the previous results of different stimuli, and that in a way has created a path that is to be traversed or actions that are to be, on it, it's horizons sometimes narrow sometimes widened, with no certainty to as to which direction it'll turn or as to how divulging will its borders be, all depended on conscience voiced the most, mere words take on form and get meaning, the justifiability of any action, dependent on the outcome, as the proof of an argument rests upon the disproof that stands on its foundation, A never-ending cycle, much more like a Mobius strip, a little twist somewhere along the path, making the entire cycle continue over again with differencing fluctuations , and these fluctuations, just one that's, seeming and coming again over and over again, the same syntax just different figureheads filling in the blanks, and one figure head changing the reality of all the consciences in questions like a virus that remains dormant and dead, having and showing no movement at all in any regards unless it reaches its host and as its host is reached, the entire spectrum is disrupted and transmuted into that which is desired by that one set of governing principles given by the action of that conscience, it being as relatively melancholy as like the settings of a circus where the jests are performed not according to a format but mostly in accordance with a shock and awe factor in mind, in that sense randomness being the utmost factor, and this conscience influenced by palpable force of want and need, not being defined in anyway, unique, no indication of what it might influence or come up with such a thing that was never even thought of might be a deterring factor in its definition, a self-imagined fear it may be, or calculation of a repetitive loss over an incidence that was predicted in the same manner, and just this thought of it, will alter its dimensions, as it being permeable there are no fix dimensions to its creation or its maintenance, but how actually it is formed, what factors influence it, what causes it to even come in existence then linger on as a gust of wind that fills a vacuum in all the unfilled occlusions , let's examine some of these aspects, in the chronological order:

A) Conception:

The very act of a conscience being created in the very first place is in most cases the aggregate action of random. changing, permeable factors such the emotional stimuli that dictates need and want, and it is influenced by trivial things such as weather, health and random incidences such as sighting a bird, looking at the growth of a tree over the years, these actions leading up to in a way a concept of serenity, that this serene atmosphere be replicated and as these events are happening in a harmonious manner events that are contradictory to this cycle are detrimental to advancement in prosperity, and as such, they are not present in this process, they should not be present elsewhere as well, thus per example a new horizon of conscience comes into existence , making things that one has not experience even if they be more industrious, be termed as, not needed and useless and even an opposition to them is created, such meaningless stimuli progresses into something transcendent, a thing non-existent, completely irrelevant, created by the action of thought, and thought itself being created by the action of minute instances

B) Formation:

With the initial action, the process that conceives it, the conscience or the new level of it is then influenced by all the preceding actions and with these preceding actions its dimensions are defined in accordance with them whereas anomalies do occur and they are more than common to say the least isolated factors have a much more severe effect in the way it is formed as they being hidden from general view create a sense that is not easily explainable for it is not predicted in that manner and that lack of foresight of how things should be in that scenario only begets to term the formation of the conscious in another manner , and this anomaly catches eye more than the subtle changes that take place, for even a little spot on a homogenous texture is more profound than greater spot on a texture of the same magnitude that takes half its characteristics , quality and quantity, it's magnitude and duration of happening is a factor that can claim more credit in the way all this is shaped than the happening of a practiced event as that which is generally known is kept at bay and that which negates it, gains more simply because of the reason that it chips away at the former's legitimacy, in retrospect, a formation of an ideal which negates a generally held notion to be true, has more detrimental or beneficial views as dependent on the perspective than a dimension that is methodically thought up but is in accordance or a slightly bit disoriented, for the general negativity bias, as shown by history has been the cause of the formation of these etiquettes more than the rational instances, no matter how controlled the environment is, the borders of it are redefined and that redefinition claims, with time legitimize, from absurdity to acceptability

C) Direction:

As the blob gathers into a fold of mass, it's in a proto-creation stage, with it being made to change and become completely different from that which it originated from and this direction of it can be changed into, anything and well, everything, the problem comes into view when it solidifies as from a gelatin goo into a concrete statue that sets a precedent for further action, the way of molding it is the easiest in its humble nascent beginnings, for, as it solidifies it gathers more foundation and that foundation forever keeps on increasing dependent on the path it has been set on, and this road prolong itself on the not by its own sheer audacity for expansion but with the action of molding that is pushing the ever hardening structure forward and forward trimming away the edges, the rough spots that in the final end the, Magnus opus, that is, is not like that which was in the formation or the that it was in the direction it started in, as the direction it travels towards is littered with the refuse of the travelers before hand and even those that have yet to travel it as the outcome, being predicted, beforehand, does more to shapes its view and aesthetics than the combined action of events acting on it, a kind of an oxymoron, that which negates it, gives it, meaning after meaning, till it becomes twice that, that which was negated in the first place, the more the dissension is, the more the fast the speed is, and the more struggles try to curb it, the more in turn expand it, the thing that which tends to destroy it in turn creates it over and over again over the action of erasing it, that which is intended the complete opposite happens as the fuel that keeps it running is the friction that tends to stop it, and this vast direction on which has been set off on, creates multitudes of different ways in the process of its running, each being a like clone with a little mutation, and little by little, bit by bit, each clone that separates from it to travel on another direction is, even though it be claimed the same with a minor difference, completely different an entity in its own regard, a paradigm, a contender that from the purpose of its furthering to the opposite of it, just a small fell swoop is all that is required when its existence is like a small cell to make it travel a wave that will take it far-far away from the coast it set off from, and to never return back to it, but towards another shore, whose existence is as prophesied and as certain as its purpose was in the beginning but no shore is ever reached, and no purpose in its prime form is ever accomplished

Quintessential premises:

All of it is as a mystery as much as its formation is a rarity, something forming out of nothing to become something that is able to turn something in turn nothing, a tale that un-tells another, such an action being performed by mere thought as thought itself is the reactive action created by the consecutive actions of different influencing factors and those influencing factors all contribute in a manner a part of their energy towards a select r a particular thought as that thought to which that energy is accumulated towards becomes a part that action in itself, ergo, thought itself is an action in reserve ready to take place, dormant, sleeping as the avalanche does only a trickle of sound a whisper is able to unleash is ferocity and all those accumulated factors acting in succession are enacted again in part and thus a new action which seems new is actually a conglomeration of all the pervious actions acting upon it like a point of convergence that need some sort of a stimuli to diverge and that divergence has the power of all those that were there in that converging point, something seeming so meaningless has such a meaningful overtone, this being the focal point of a further happening, meaning to think is in a way to do, and to do is the implementation of thought that was created by this cycle forever continuing, and this continuation is further fueled by the repetitive actions that might seem to hinder it but all actions therefore a part of its progress so and so that everything is futile when it comes to negating a set principle for all of that negation serves in giving it a more firm foundation the only sure way to stop is to instead of negating it, negate its very existence, but would that negation not give it more power than before that it is so powerful all together that such an action as to completely stop thinking about it is needed for it to not exist for a brief moment? Like a pigeon closing its eye as the cat is about to strike, with all these in perspective a simple thought that once comes in mind is the sole perpetrator of all the succeeding action that might be taken as a simple thought alters that moment in which it was conceived, that moment in a chronographic perspective alters all other moments and all other moments of a select individuals being altered has or in part some effect on another individual on whom the same case applies their life being altered by the thoughts of others around them, even though not directly expressed this mere action of thinking being more powerful than a direct action based on the thinking likewise, meaning a thing that cannot be destroyed is more powerful than all those actions even if in a congregation taken together as that which is clearly evident is able to be stopped whereas that which does not have a clear starting or an ending is infinite or absolute, terming something actually terms it in that manner and fits it into that category and for an idea to be all powerful it must not let itself be boxed in a faction or associated as belonging to such, it should have such dynamics that it can originate and compliment other ideas but their effect on it is negligible and that is done just by its grandiose claim of it being unquestionable and as that unquestionable quality comes into play that it cannot be in any way altered or attempts to alter it are futile as it has more power to do, change, make or break than all other ideals combined, it being obstinately stubborn, is the main reason that gives it the power to shape the vast horizons of conscience to its will either expanding them immensely, contracting them or maintain, giving legitimacy to that which is already established, all by the ideal in itself giving itself a claim of perfection , for perfection is just a perception and if an idea can only be understood or is claimed to be understood through a lens of completely purity or perfection than all other attempts to negate it or provide evidences no matter how powerful or coherent they are, are of no match against it, as it leaps over the barriers of rationality and when rationality is disregarded it doesn't really matter what the opposing idea has to claim, as that idea in itself is self-sufficient a living entity, if one may, whose death is possible only by another claiming such a trait and gathering more support than its predecessor, the majority having authority

Conjectures being created in the heat of the moment or the from the residue of it, can gather mass at an unprecedented rate and it all depends on how the factors in accordance to that

reaction, sometimes a simple act can have enormous effects if a small disliking to it is exacerbated to the point of a vehement contention, an attitude against or for it, can alter the entire meaning if the original result had or intended none so whatever, the events after the one that has preceded are more crucial in its maintenance or destruction as the nascent feelings are mutable and this mutable nature can change it, shape it in forms that were in no way even hinted by it only because the acting forcing are the resultant or the conducive factors to that which the residue is taking the form of, and vice versa a very well thought up mode of action will dissipate in an instant if the factors around it are in a state of indifference or if it is unable to entertain or the arouse the momentary temper which is at high during the point in which it is mentioned and/or created

But what actually constitute ideals those that are lumped together form a conscience? What are these elements? Is there even a definition that defines them? Or this vagueness is beyond comprehension or is perhaps so that there is an underlying factor a common overtone that's is or manifests its self as that characteristic which is common

i)   Appeal to generality:

The foremost observable trait in any ideal that is set up is that there is a somewhat connection to the happenings around it, something that entices and allures in whatever manner it may please to do so but at the same time it being vague enough to classify certain workings into a criteria and on the other hand it is precise enough to perfectly fit with that assumed presumption, a mix or a blend of such elements is found, and that mix is on the degree of equilibrium with the things at large giving also a sense of belonging and progressing or regressing further a set of thought, this appeal to the masses is what gets it attention that which makes it take a hold in the crowd making them as such a scaffold to stand on, and this scaffolding serves as an obelisk to which the masses gather see in it a forecast of what their own thought of version it is going to further and instead of it being moved by and along with the crowd the crowd starts to move with it, as it shambles across with its shaky cadaver and as it sprawls with life with everyone's association with it, in fact this appeal to generality is powerful that with it people are rallied behind it on the pretense that it is already a form of that which exists but just in a better shape and this discourse of regarding it the same but changed old but new, contradictory forms associated with whatever version one pleases of think of it as, and in turn they or it being changed gradually, and this amalgamation of change is so subtle yet so very noticeable that it is hard to distinguish which are the wishes which have come to be associated with it or which are its actual points which gave it credibility in the first place just by retaining its concept of appeal to masses it can be morphed into any shape that is seen fit, being completely new and yet still seeming as though it has not changed even in the least bit and this macabre façade will give it a liking and yet this liking will be in contradiction to that which was abhorred and or dejected in the first place the want being changed without one ever knowing that it was changed in the first place with gradual progression of time it goes through different versions and it being in public light completely that is an unsure surety that it cannot change as it is being monitored completely whereas this thinking is the very cause that it changes the most right under the noses of the masses without them even finding out until it's too late, and when this certainty shatters it is regarded that the view was wrong since the beginning and not the case that all the observers were deluded completely

ii) A sense of correctness

There is an inherent need of validation, that one's actions are not, nor are going to be a cause of his isolation, and this craving that comes with it, is satisfied by, an approval that is given by thought that which one pursues or is doing is somewhat justified and with this notion in mind there comes a sense of liberation that at least ones actions cannot in a later date be held against him and with this view in mind, the ability to do that which seemed particularly odd or uncomfortable becomes a breeze, that it can be so easily done as there exists a moral backing from one's self, and this backing can take one to heights previously held too high, and this sense of correctness forks into various paths succeedingly, that if one action is justified the resultant actions that will result from it are justified as well, a long chain has started, in which only the first link which joins it to some common standing is the only point worthy of validation and as it is validated by being attached to common morality than all further happenings resulting from it are too as well, this fallacy or undeniable logic is or can be classified as the root which goes deeper and deeper on the starting pretext, as this non-existent feeling that one is on the right path can be dangerously destructive or highly progressive depending on what the society has given moral standing to, feats of great vigor can be easily accomplished and sometimes feats of terrible atrocity are overlooked as being a necessary evil, a small point, that arises from whatever reason it may, if not nipped in the bud can grow into such a big tree that it can even overshadow the moral group that gave it validation in the first place, becoming so out of hand or un-trim-able that, the invention overpowers the inventor and when this has happened it goes beyond all power that can stop or destroy it easily in the beginning, a creation of a monster, or an arch-angel depending on either it benefits or depreciates, colossal eminence at the end just by the sheerness

of it being accepted, and this colossus ever-growing and being built on the notion that the life

it'll gain will be the answer of the wishes of the masses, but the masses that benefit by it are most

certainly a not the ones that envision it or give it the go ahead, instead a different class reaps the

rewards of the risks that come with it as the acceptance that was given to it was from a time

period in which it was okay, but when it gains momentum it might find itself where there it

might not be accepted but the culmination of the previous backing give it more reason or is made

to be fit into the jigsaw puzzle of the time it has been hurled or moved into

iii) Heat of the moment

Another characteristic highly common with the creation of any ideal is that it generally arises due to a conflict or an instance of disagreement which in turn makes the air of opposition give it a momentum, it arising merely due to some sort of conflict or a disagreement on one's part and is it accumulates, that air of opposition, it can transform itself into a gust that can even turn into a tornado, all depending on how sentimental that movement in which it came into being was, if that moment was somehow appealing to one's honor that such an view point came into being it might be then supported even more ardently as that tempo, the saying of it that is, translates into the character of the one that mad it come into light in the first place, that persons or groups legitimacy tied to a promise they made of their own accord to prove a point or their mettle, and an inability to do so creates an environment of frustration that which mutates it further as ideals coming into existence due to this reason are more permeable and susceptible to change as their existence was just hot air and nothing more, but going back on it, that is going back on one's word, removes one from feeling a sense of correctness or identification with generality as the outer appearance of the society is made to reflect a ray of truth and honesty that which at is best a form of utopia and at its worst the average life of a citizen and nothing less, with such pretense to be countered it is to be noted that this self-created floating balloon will be made to seem more heavier or as one with more legitimacy and this hot air being constantly filled in it will most certainly make it blow in ones face as these ideals are purely in majority of the cases just conjecture and not a thought up outcome that was to be selected if the arguments were to go this far and with such haste in selection there is not even a path for it that is considered instead just a thought up outcome in which the one making such claim is somehow superior by the magnanimity of that claim likewise the opposing party or the one which is made to feel inferior on which claim the ideal is made in the first place and for its support, the imaginary scenario of a self-selected game in which the victor is the one making the most outrageous claim is to be, and as the haze of that hot air dies, it becomes clearly evident that this claim was based in a time that in some manner is not valid but on the contrary if a claim is made in such an instance and the party that makes it has the means and wit to take it to fruition the most absurd action will gain validity and justification having more power to surpass the previous three types of ideals

iv)   Opportunity of perseverance:

The idea of not letting oneself being carried by the flood of sameness, a way of preserving one's individuality while not being the black sheep nor being an outcast something that one can call uniquely theirs and at the same it identifies with the society as not being something that can be deemed a deterrent to its progress that one can apply this to oneself be unique and be the same at the same time, an oxymoron, if you will, and it also in that moment giving one a perceived notion of opposition that is in clash not with their being but with their display of perfection giving an ego boost, that their character is subject to envy as they are somewhat scorned by those that cannot be like them or cannot act on that ideal to become like them, even if that ideal is nothing but just a perception or a thing that entices their adrenaline and tells them that they will not only be a part of society but will be a different figure unlike others while not fully blending in as much so as to disappear nor not being that prominent that be held as an object of jest, being in a state of equilibrium between the two, being better and yet not crossing not any unspoken boundaries, freeing one with a little opposition as to legitimize their claim to be valid even if it may be not so, only with a little force that stands against it will it be given the feel that it is somehow worthy of pursuit, and in this process one can form their identity and enhance it as they see fit being something that is befitting of praise and that praise being given its rightful due with an envious demeanor in existence against it, as one strives to make their mark, and when they are part of a group or society that gives them individuality in some transcendent terms by being a part of it, this action on their part as promulgated by the ideal, gives itself a means of propagation, making it self-sufficient as one feels being able to preserve themselves so can others do the same by following that previous demeanor and in turn giving the one following it more reason to be different yet belong to the same class, such a factor being a main contributor in its promotion , as it relieves other of the burden of being helpless by giving them power to battle against a most likely non prevailing opposition in whose defense they are themselves the champion for they are themselves the referee

v)   Escape from the past

Being held back or tied down by events that are completely out of ones controls puts one into a bondage from which there is no way of visibly escaping, and this prison that holds down their thoughts limiting in thinking ergo from doing that which they'd like to do, supersedes all form of physical slavery that one can experience, bondage of the mind is the one where there is no emancipation and when an ideal appeals to it, that one can get out, free themselves, from the specter that comes after them from the past, the possession that cannot be rid by a simple exorcism, and this ideal telling them that they are free, absolved of their wrongdoing, all that they have done they are bereft of its consequences, that no further proceeding or effects that have been set in motion by that pervious action of theirs will not change them in any way, than that ideal becomes a way of their freedom a key of the door that leads them out of the dungeon that they are trapped in, the labyrinth riddled with their mistakes that they see at every turn and come back to the place over and over again as if they were lost in it, that ideal being the basis of something that atones a person, and to be rid of all that which were detrimental to a person is like starting with a new slate, being born again, as some groups claim also, this quality of redeeming being present in the ideal or it being the ideal itself gives it qualities tantamount to resuscitation, resuscitation of the dead husk of the past that was free of the actions whose reactions are being suffered, that return to that previous state, the longing of getting away leaving it all behind starting anew , but without actually leaving all that one has, at the same time having to have that what the current state has to offer all that one wants or has stocked up and also ridding of all the residue that has gathered upon all the possessions at hand with such an outcome being offered just by adherence to that ideal, there is no question of its self-righteous authenticity, that one absolves another of the illogic behind their deeds is in itself cleared of giving an explanation that explains the moral authority it has to absolve another in the first place, the aspect of it giving while not having anything to give, makes it's treasury a limitless chest laden with gold, as there is no counter or weight to pit against it or to measure how much is it's giving capacity as it wipes away the that feeling of another like it was never in the first place with its thesaurus of virtues and wisdom that "supersede" human intellect, even if it is a byproduct of the factor it surpasses in the first place

Perils:

With all these tales being told, it becomes known, that ideals that can be formed in the heat of the moment, due to the action or remembrance of a past event, calculated demeanor or simply as a means of escape, and with it they, with further workings become conglomerated with the environmental factors prevailing during the time of their formation and with each passing day, they by their sheer claim of excellence gain legitimacy and this legitimacy gained is further intensified with the support of others, or simply it is as valid as the number of people that back it, the number of followers making it have some sort of a reason to strut around as the resultant factor of thought cannot get better than it, to sum these workings, what is an ideal but a collection of whims and wants, and what is conscience itself? Except their aggregate, such trivialities changing complete parameters of thought defining what is right and what is wrong and these definitions being so concrete that these notions give more preference to what they have to same even though the opposing argument is created in the same manner the same mode of conveyance and the same environmental factors prevailing or at least the same magnitude is, and the conscience that is developed from it encompasses or claims to encompass all other ideals that will be made, such absurd claims are the reason that give it an iron will power to do so, without doing so, claiming to be transcendent not affected by worldly woes and with this action they are completely exempt from the consequences of their own and the repercussions their mode of judgment will have on others, conscience can be regarded as just a tool, a tool that can forge and chip away from the statues of our being, simple thought can influence magnanimous elements like landscapes, something that can start in such an innocent manner can come to become powerful beyond reproach, from humble beginning to a mighty end, that is, of the elements it acts upon and it's action being as powerful as the amount of extra worldly character that it associates with its own self, with this being said, it is right to assume that for an empire to crumble it's ideals must lose validation and that validation can only be done by a conscience that is against it but against it in a way that the conflict is not direct, that the one it opposes is too meaningless to be even considered and that conscience being opposed is rather a small pawn in the ocean of generality it seeks to define, a mere foam on the sea that has merit being washed away by the new dimensions it seeks to propose and the dimensions can be narrow more so than the element that's under opposition, the ideals themselves giving power to the conscience that is being formed by their attitude of obstinate diligence in the face of odds which are rife around its nascent beginnings, the real paradox is the power that it has of influence over the prevailing masses and that influence is more strengthened when the concerned party is made to feel completely helpless that no amount of effort on their part is going to solve even a part of the problems that are to come for the newly made conscience is the only solution the only key that'll unlock the gates of bliss, only when one surrenders to it will one be able to live up to or defend oneself from all other threats as this feeling of helplessness is what compels a person in the first place to seek a means of reassurance that thing will turn out alright where as in fact things in general remain in the same homogenous state as they were with little variations owing to that there are no severe external factors that can completely alter the course of their running, when problems are made out of thin air whose solutions are present in the same medium, then the thought that one gives to that conscience is the backbone which makes it keep encompassing further and further the life and way of thinking of the concerned individual, as it only exists when there is a degree of attention paid to it otherwise ideals with a perfect or a near so, vision of their perceived future succumb to idleness and eventually disappear for they were not taken into consideration or they were not sufficiently excitable or was unable to arouse activity in the dorsolateral prefrontal cortex, to be technical, and for that reason alone was not merited a minute of wise thought as to the implications of its implementation and with this reason and this reason alone many ideals that could've formed a working system progressive and not as debilitating as the current accepted norm, that might've caused a flourishing of creative expression more so than that which is at best not discriminated against would've been a part of that which is acceptable or more so even propagated as more harm been done to the human psyche by determining that some elements are free from deductive results of thought, they they are infallible, such attitude has deterred progress that with the principle of cause and effect would have multiplied more than a thousand folds and this limiting mindset can only be altered when, it , the end of a conscience be regarded as a new beginning instead of an unchartered territory that which one may try to surpass would only end up in peril whereas its conquest might unlock a treasure of wisdom that could be termed as something never before seen, but the real question is how can it be done, how can one distance itself from the limited mindset that is contained in the cages of uncertainty, that only doubt limits free flow of ideas, what can be the focal point or the point of convergence from where one can be neutral as well as take a side, but most importantly how will that point occur that one might be able to do so

1) Disassociation

To be fully able to comprehend or understand a situation one should one have personal stake in it, for when that happens, the happenings of that event and that which a person wants to happen by it, get intertwined and thus, one is caught in the web of dependency, and being able to escape or find anew, or build one, that is, a new path, a new ordeal, one must completely remove or at least picture himself in an environment that is separate from that condition and when one thinks of the limits of the limits of that conscience as not bin ding upon him, then can he rightly know the difference between what he wants and what he is being made to want, separation, even in any sense even if it be a trivial slanting perception, opens up paths, previously thought non-traversable, and when one is not made to follow that which he sees fit but something that can be set in motion that only whose events will be to his liking, he gets a sense of power as well, power to control and manipulate without doing so, gaining results without having anything concrete that will deduce them in the first place, only when is on an elevated surface can be fully see how uneven the surface is, not vice versa and this trait of distancing oneself from an ordeal that one wishes to change/negate then things start to become clear, that there is more to a picture than previously thought, the big picture becomes somewhat clear than it was or aspects of it are seen that were not considered drawn at all, but when one considers their self a part of it, that the definitions defined by that conscience are somewhat relevant and leaving them or choosing to ignore them will have indebt oneself to a guilty conscience or social repercussions than the desired state is not reached that one could wish for it be, the view are amalgamated to account for any discrepancies that are in part or at all felt and one is limited or a more exact label, chained, by his own mind of what can and not be done and this state of being in bondage prevents one from fully realizing his or her potential as, being limited to just the scope that which the conscience one has or was subliminally yet forcefully been adhered to, and the only mode of liberation is thinking of something that is, existent, yes, but one that can only affect a person if that person allows themselves to be affected or influenced by it and all other modes of pressure to get one to or be under its wing are futile unless the person himself does not allow it to be so, with this mindset freedom from events or circumstance can be gained on the pretext that they were something in a time period and they will only be so again if one replicates that period again

2) Contemplation

As seeming trivial as it might sound but just trying to find the end limits or confines from which a conscience cannot progress or its influence ends might so cause to replicate that exact thought process simply by the act of looking at the defines defined by it, making it lose all validity by trying to find what actually is that which gives it validity in the first place a reverse-tinker bell effect, in which the more trust is given to an ideal the more it is lost in turn as the act of trusting something is going right , attention towards it is tend to be lost and as it wanes away, the actions that it was doing perfectly well under monitored circumstance became disordered and are disoriented from the original path, and this simplicity, that is from the thought process of finding legitimacy for its claims but when it cannot be found for it was most certainly not there in the first place as, the horizons of a conscience are littered with stars that are mistaken for its moons, and blind adherence can only last so long, until abruptly collapsing upon itself and this collapse removes all splendor that it might have gained or propagated through the use of its infallible right to govern or dictate by the word of its own mouth, one slip in it, makes all other claims by it questionable and when those questions become profound and more profound that the sheer number of them can outweigh all answers that it might pose in its defense, and this abundance of questions even though answerable, but just one slip in between and all the hard work in its defense cannot attain fruition, and is, without a doubt, In vain and this sort of thinking just contemplating, over and over again the meaning and the outcome can seldom give it more legitimacy, as the natural tendency to find flaws to ensure a smooth survival of the species and as the very change is the law of nature and the answers as being unchangeable for they support the very basic principles promulgated by that conscience to distinguish between its own aims and wrong, and simply by posing questions and being undeterred in their magnitude not Lessing the frequency or the topics about it that it touches, will erode away from it the balance as the fixed shoreline is eroded away, thus, if one wants to make for them or in general for others a rule or a path to be followed, he need only sit in a corner and think and just think over and over again, giving legitimacy to his own claims and then as those claims will clash again the previous dominating force, the friction will cause both to come into light and be in retrospect to the original circumstance to which the opposing conscience has been formulated, either for a means of escape of continuity of the desired norms

3) Action

Sometimes it so happens, that events that pertain to the implementation of the oh so idealistically praised perfect mode of execution of certain events, fail drastically when the moment arrives, as that which looks good on paper hasn't tasted the dust from outside, and when such happens, or merely one thinks of starting its implementation the events unfold completely in contradiction to the way they have been said to happen and every contradiction further removes it's claim of being all powerful, the confines of a conscience that is, and as most certainly, it is envisioned in a state of either a perceived utopia or a dystopia and this state is limited to the extreme conditions that do not exist in actual-actuality and this non-existence of such circumstance do tend to replicate their own scenario of being into the conscience that taps into them by classifying them in a manner of its own liking and thus is itself classified by the resultant forces, a conscience is only as good as it's successful intellectual exploits, the more it can highlight a certain problem rather than give a better solution makes it's "solution" seem better with consistent attacks of falsehood and deception on the one which it seeks to negate, but when it comes to actions or just trying to envision it in a scenario where its aspects are rationally implemented there are many loopholes found and by default with its obstinate attitude of magnanimity it beclouds itself to evident flaws of its own, and these substantial claims crucial for successful implementation show how very perfect they are, action is more harmful to a select group of ideals than the their retort for as much as they are rejected they have a claim that their workings are far superior than others and it simply is a defense mechanism by preceding institutions to curb progress or their version of it, but, when it actually is shown that it is simply bloated air with no backing of anything that translates into viable in reality ergo signaling that It is just good in the books or a decorum by which one can strut around leisurely but nothing more so is any way of use for it be enhance

one's endeavors or profit them likewise, and this non-attainment of any benefited, the state of

being completely unrequited devotion clearly tells how absurd it all is for it simple conjecture

sugar coated with the foretelling of great order or maintenance of likewise, this action or trying

to act upon it makes one disillusioned from its promises, by finally lifting the shroud that

prevented one from seeing all the evident shortfalls or seeing that it itself is but that, it is rightly

said action is the enemy of thought, for it limits more, than all opposing argumentation against it

can in anyway

4) Critique

It sometimes so happen that a certain conscience has limits defined which are in a manner incomprehensible that all forms of logic fails against them, as their unquestionable logic is supported by the doctrine of non-questionability that as it is defined as so powerful and absolute that even thinking of questioning it is an attack at it head on and such an attack is detrimental to the peace and wellbeing of all those concerned in such cases the only way one can dissociate themselves from it is by, resorting to a manner of negation, simply saying that is not worth it or just being critical of its aspects and this act of being critical tends to make it loose its value in the eyes of the person that is going against it and that act of judging it in a manner that its worth is like that of an ordinary person subject to opinion and change, its controlling power tends to lose its value as ridicule takes away any notions of intellectual persuasion it had, its absurd points which were given an element of its focal strength by deeming them as the sole point that determines whether it is of any value or not is disregarded as a fool's errand, simple delusion and this opinion is voiced dramatically in a manner noticeable , just saying that it deserves nothing nor is it of any importance that which is assigned to it and the actions purported to it of being the only answer is completely bonkers, with its points being deterred by an influx of non-conformity and an attitude of it being ignored as just part of a play or a jest, that has gained a bit too much notice because of its talks about stuff that it has made up on its own, the problems its very existence create and it in turn tries to correct those problems which were never there but its act of existence made them so by giving solutions that are not needed and in that process negating other modes of acceptability of conflict resolution over its own by its demeanor of not listening or being adaptable to change and with these workings being under great pressure or being made a part of something that is taken in a light manner, instead of vehemently opposed as opposition on that level tends to give it more legitimacy than to take it away from it as in a rational attack points are highlighted which are logical in nature but completely opposite to that which it propagates and those points are taken in their opposing form as something that was already a part of it, even though widespread critique can out rightly break a conscience's hold on the minds, a little slip in it can strengthen it further than it already was by giving it an outlook that it is too powerful and the people who are opposed to it as merely resisting it as they are the ones defined as those who profit unjustly on another's expense creating an environment of its adherents in subjugated state, ergo, critique if handled and given where it's due with the right blend of logic and absurdness can prove to give a more fatal blow than a head on tackle trying to force it down

5) Disregard

Another sure way to distance oneself from the confines of the defined manner of life is to simply ignore it, the conceptual paradigm of its values is only limited to thought and when there is no such action that determines or even sees that it is in a form existent it tends to lose its meaning, like an event that hasn't happened, with disregard comes a much more powerful notion of freedom as when one does not consider anything- anything at all then there are no forces that can limit its future workings as the person in question has refused to see such happenings on the path ahead, even though they are not, just the simple thought of them being there is cause enough for hindrance, the prison of the mind is the most secure to escape from, and the pages of the conscience are written with the ramblings of the loudest mind, as when in a state of calmness all voice is shut out, so can it be the case for this occurrence as well, just not thinking of it, regarding it as a question not worth talking about, a conjecture or a waste of time, no matter how valid or powerful it may be, just not thinking of it will make it disappear altogether at its action of influencing a person just by it being there, disregard is the most strongest attack, as it is an attack which is not exactly so in that sense, simply not seeing it, makes it be there no more, for the ideals are mostly supported by the ones that oppose them, but when one idea is either two absurd or two ingenious to be understood if no opposition is there for it, it just vanishes from the thin air it came from, just by trying to shut it out, one can actually shut it out, the human mind the originator and in itself the destroyer of entire coming worlds just with power of further pursuing engaging as to the point it envelopes the being and it makes it act accordingly or if the being is completely unaffected by it by careful carelessness of not regarding any aspect of it, like a stray thought that is gone without any remorse longing it to come back, so does happen with it too, it is no more to behold and there is no one there to behold it, an ideal being immensely dictating, logical and resonating but when there is nothing that can reciprocate these very traits nor even be listen to them, all of it fades away from the nothingness it came, disregard being the most efficient and the most power depleting tool in liberating one from the confines of a conscience

6) Acceptance

Even though it'll feel as a counterproductive measure when one tries to distance and liberate themselves from the confines of a defined conscience, but, when the conscience is just too strong to negate or even disregard, it is much more advisable that one accepts it just that it be not a force in opposition to that party and with acceptance one not only becomes a part of the massive unutilized crowd, he also doesn't have to worry about going against the very institutions put forth by it, and thus by accepting it, one is more easily free, if that acceptance is just so an outwardly one and has no concrete properties, then not will he have support of the denizens residing in the cavern created by this conscience he will also be able to propagate his own view by deeming them a part of the conscience itself by the claim of deducing further results or morphing the defined aspects into something more meaningful, even in that meaning turns out gradually to be completely against it, the trick is not be, or have a general negative attitude towards the points being altered little by little, bit by bit, by superficially accepting that is projecting an image of accepting it, it becomes much more easy to do as one pleases as they are perceived as a threat to society as they appear to be a loyal subject of the ideals they are so subversively eroding or cleansing themselves of the erosion that is the ideals placed upon them in the first place, to appear helpless removes one from the image of being a potential threat, as that who is down itself can do no good to oneself, and is not in any position to do bad or the actions that have been termed bad as to keep that helpless person in that position of helplessness or so preserve order by breaking the legs and ensuring that an interrupted supply of crutches and for the maintenance of that supply necessary action of crippling all those able to not run at an outpacing speed or their version of propagating a wellness that gives complete certainty that one walk without having to worry about the support being broken as it is abundant and in abundant supply, to just show that one's guard is down, and let those ideals appear as, to others that is, dominant, and then more a person works with those ideals displaying a portrait of his character the more he is regarded as in line with the limits of that society, but this method of acceptance can, if the resolution is not strong, make one become an adherent as with this mode of action it's influence increases tenfold over the concerned group as living two separate identities can cause an eventual conglomeration, this point should only be used as a last resort as a means of emancipation if the will is not strong enough to face the might of the opposing odds

Riposte

With these happenings well defined it is evident that the entire system of a conscience has stemmed from the notions of whims and conjectures and these succeeding events give it power and validation which in turn makes the point environed at first without any backdrop seem like the only sustainable mode of discourse simply by the act of it arousing the senses or creating a sense of being under threat from consequences that will result without acknowledging it and this Mobius strip logic becomes self-sustaining to allow itself continue by exploiting the apparent weakness or the weakness that are made simply appear, even though conscience itself is a tool which gives framework or molds a specific group or body of individuals into united body by use of different tactics of lure, even if the courses which are required to be pledged allegiance to can be quite productive and innocent at best, but the means that are gradually em0ployed by the human psyche to attain an end which is perceived to be productive and helpful to the overall rate of general satisfaction but the population included in that scale of generality is quite and/or quite minute depending on which way it is looked at, a conscience can either deter or advance the progress of any given society dependent to what level it can be encompassing, simple endeavors when backed by a notion of tremendous gain can achieve results previously thought not even conceivable all these depends on how well calculated the defines of a conscience are, the more micromanaging it is, the more productive it will be , but the timeframe of its functionality becomes rather small, even if it will claim otherwise where as those with such extended or poorly defined horizons that the sun of a new epoch can dawn before it is understood in anyway, gets with it associated, some sort of characteristic of honor, a characteristic of endurance that it has manifested by retaining its core principals or the principals that are attributed to it at the end of any given cycle of loss or success it has gone through, all these transcendent aspects assigned to the trivialities that are made into an idealist form of life, these all coming from the biological aspects of assessing the environment around a sentient being or if taken in the light of the conscience which makes the psyche independent and omnipotent, on which it stakes its very claim of power, as being something that actually occupies a vessel instead of it being the other way around and this thinking has digressed into paths of perfections as attainable, deeming humans as somewhat different from other creatures, that they have the ability to do so that other organisms cannot and these defines set by a conscience for a consciousness to assess the favorable and not so favorable aspects of any given circumstance so that it can continue in its state so a desirable end, that most certainly never comes in the manner described, be achieved, but the real quandary with respect to all these arguments is whether, the limits of conscience upon a conscious have merit or not, is consciences a self-sustaining entity, that retains its own on its very own that needs guidance as to how, when and why it must do, what it has ought to do, or is consciousness a creation or an agent of the biological systems put forth to determine how on the behalf of, or acting in the favor of the body it must work, that simply the biological entity continue to exist, even as this question the very basis of, if things be taken into the light of idealism as they are construable by minds of individuals who having the same exact system of workings, somehow know better and are entitled to implement their views on others, on the basis they know better, simply because that which is put forth says that they know better, an inescapable logic, even if this question can be answered a further dilemma comes into existence if the notions are all that power in whatever direction they come, which view should be accepted if both are valid in their own self-professed light, and neither is accepting of the other's argument, can both these stand together parallel without merging into another and causing a jumbled incomplete version that not fully answers anything, being broken in its workings continue to dictate the streams of validation and where they should be made to flow, or making the streams by its own self of which it likewise gives direction, without there actually being any streams nor there being no visible way to give it direction either, and where the other is doing the same but in the manner opposed to it, both standing on nothingness and speculation by both of them on the others vacancy is what makes a mirage appear only visible from the point they stand at, but with all the human collective consciousness, is it not very ironic that the agreement on their workings and origination is still non-agreeable, with all human progress and its unrivaled achievements, the very basis through which all have been made able to reach a standard which the best or the ones thought of as best have achieved, should consciousness be regarded just as an extension of the bodily systems to ensure their nourishment or should there be an extra worldly aspect which classifies as being absolute and undeterrable in its resolution, even if that answer be somewhat contradictory, should a previous outcome be regarded as all encompassing? The human has made able one to decide the parameters of good and bad vis-à-vis the answer lies in, not what is, but, what should be, the competent authority in determining the extensions of sentient progress lies in the direction that's antithetical to the one that's prevenient.